SECOND BOOK OF ETHIOPIAN MACCABEES

Translated by: D.P. Curtin
Assisted by: Bekele Tesfaye
Edited by: Jessica Curtin

Dalcassian Publishing Company
PHILADELPHIA, PA

SECOND BOOK OF ETHIOPIAN MACCABEES

Copyright @ 2023 Dalcassian Publishing Company

All rights reserved. No part of this publication may be reproduced, distributed, or transmitted in any form or by any means, including photocopying, recording, or other electronic or mechanical methods, without the prior written permission of the publisher, except in the case of brief quotations embodied in critical reviews and certain other non-commercial uses permitted by copyright law. For permission request, write to Dalcassian Publishing Company at dalcassianpublishing at gmail.com

ISBN: 979-8-8692-1148-4 (Paperback)

Library of Congress Control Number:
Author: Curtin, D.P. (1985-)

Printed by Ingram Content Group, 1 Ingram Blvd, La Vergne, Tennessee

First printing edition 2023.

SECOND BOOK OF ETHIOPIAN MACCABEES

SECOND BOOK OF ETHIOPIAN MACCABEES

SECOND BOOK OF ETHIOPIAN MACCABEES

CHAPTER I

1:1   This is the book of Maccabeus, who found Israel in Mesopotamia and slew them there, beginning with Jabbok[1] up to the center of Jerusalem. He laid waste to that country.

1:2   Since the Syrians, Edomites, and Amalekites were as kin to Maccabeus, the man from Moab who laid waste the land of Jerusalem, they camped from the valleys of Samaria to the center of Jerusalem and in all her far-reaching lands.

1:3   They slew all those who fled from them in battle, sparing only a select few.

1:4   In that day, the children of Israel did wrong, and [God] raised up the man from Moab[2], Maccabeus, against them, and he slew them with his sword.

1:5   Thereafter, the people, who were enemies of the Lord, boasted against the dignity of His nation, and they praised their crimes.

1:6   The people of Philistinia[3] and Edom were encamped, as [the Lord] had sent them forth, for they feigned the word of the Lord, and they wreaked havoc on the Lord's nation.

1:7   Now, the country of Maccabeus was Ramath[4], that is in the land of Moab.

---

[1] This is a tributary river of the Jordan, a region that was historically associated with the kingdom of Ammon (Deut. 2:37). Today it is better known as the Zarqa river. This specific place name might suggest that this military personality (assuming that they were historical) had a power based on the Jabbok river, which in the Hellenic period would have likely been Jerash, also known as 'Antioch on the Chrysorrhoas'. This would then explain the confabulation of personalities as this city was allegedly chartered by King Antiochus IV.

[2] This connection with Moab is curious, as Moabite culture was in considerable decline during the Hellenic period. Perhaps this is a confabulation of identity with the famous Tobiad family who were from the Transjordan region in the 2nd century BC.

[3] Famously, the Philistines as a distinct ethnographic people had been destroyed for several centuries by the time of the Maccabean revolt in 168 BC.

[4] There are multiple places called Ramath, albeit none of them in the land of Moab. There is Ramath Mizpeh (Josh. 13:26), and Ramath of the South (Josh. 19:8), and Ramath Lehi (Josh. 15:17). More likely, this is the Ramath noted frequently in 1 Samuel (2:11, 7:17, 8:4, 15:34, 16:13, 19:18-22).

SECOND BOOK OF ETHIOPIAN MACCABEES

1:8 He arose from his country in strength, and they made oaths to him.

1:9 [His Army] camped in the region of Gilboa[5], that is between Mesopotamia and Syria, so that they might lay waste to the Lord's nation.

1:10 There [Maccabeus] begged the Amalekites and Philistines, giving them hoards of gold and silver, chariots and horses, so they might be accomplices to his crime.

1:11 They all assembled together and crushed the fortress, and the blood of those who resided in it flowed like water[6].

1:12 And Jerusalem they made into a barn, and his voice was heard within it.

1:13 He committed all of the acts of abomination which are offensive to the Lord, and they polluted the nation of the Lord that was formerly filled with praise and dignity.

1:14 [His army] robbed orphans and widows, for they had no fear of the Lord, and did as Satan[7] had taught them.

1:15 The Lord, who knows the hearts and minds of mankind, was disturbed, for they sliced open the babes out of their mothers' wombs[8].

1:16 And they then returned to their country jubilant in the sight of the evil they had worked against the Lord's children, taking with them the plunder from that noble land.

1:17 When they returned to their house, they made merry with songs and clapping.

---

[5] A famous mountain range in northern Israel. It was the site of the famous defeat of King Saul by the Philistines (1 Sam. 31:1,8; 2 Sam. 1:16; 1 Chr. 10:1).
[6] The sacking of this fortress in the former Moabite dominion is perhaps the same as the city sacked by Judas Maccabee elsewhere (1 Macc. 5:35).
[7] The appearance of the personality of Satan here is sentinel, as this character is granted no prologue by the author, who assumes that the audience is already familiar with their cosmological and moral role.
[8] This sounds akin to the canonical account in 2 Macc. 5:11-14

CHAPTER II

2:1 The prophet who was called 'Rei'[9] spoke to the king: "Rejoice today, for now is the time when delight can be observed.

2:2 The Lord, whom Israel glorifies, will send down His vengeance to destroy you in chastisement that you can have no doubt of.

2:3 Will you say: 'my horses are swift, and I will escape by fleeing?'

2:4 As for me, I will tell you, those who will stalk you are swifter than vultures. You will not escape from the judgment of the Lord, and desolation will fall upon you.

2:5 Will you say: 'I am dressed in clothes of iron and I cannot be harmed by the bow-string or the flinging of spears'?

2:6 The Lord who grants dignity to Israel has said: 'It is not by the flinging of spears that I will take My vengeance and decimate you.'

2:7 He said: 'I will bring down upon you diseases of the heart, stinging, and gout, that are worse and sharper than the spear of the bow. Still it is not by this that I shall take My vengeance and destroy you.

2:8 You have made My wrath arise, and I shall bring you diseased hearts, and you will find no one to give you aid.

2:9 Moreover, you will not escape from My power until I lay waste to all those who call upon your name in this world.

2:10 Since you have hardened your heart and raised your hard against My nation, I will move quickly to cast this upon you like that of the blinking of an eye.

2:11 You will know Me, that I am your Creator, when you come before Me, just like the grass that is consumed by the fire blown by the wind.

2:12 You are like the dust that the winds blow about and scatter upon the Earth, you are as this to Me.

---

[9] This is a relatively unfamiliar name because of the way that it is transliterated. It appears to be the closest to the biblical 'Rei' (1 Ki. 1:8), although this is not entirely clear.

SECOND BOOK OF ETHIOPIAN MACCABEES

2:13   For you have made My wrath arise, as you have not known your Creator.

2:14   I will turn away from all of your people, nor will I preserve him who smashed this fortress.'

2:15   Now, repent from all of your sins that you have worked. If you have repented from your sins and offer supplication in mourning and weeping before the Lord, and if you ask of Him with a clear heart, the Lord will forgive you of all your transgressions that you have worked before Him."

2:16   From this Maccabeus put dust upon his head and mourned before the Lord because of his transgressions, for the Lord had become displeased by him.

2:17   For His eyes are open and He does not look away; and His ears are listening, and He does not ignore.

2:18   He does not utter a false word, and He moves quickly all at once; for the Lord knows of the chastisement that has been spoken in the words of the prophet.

2:19   [Maccabeus] threw off his clothes and wore sackcloth and placed dust upon his head.

2:20   He cried and wept before the Lord His creator because of the sins of his hands.

CHAPTER III

3:1   The prophet then came from Ramath, and told [Maccabeus], as Ramath of Moab is near to Syria[10].

3:2   [The king] dug a pit and went into it up unto his neck and wept hard tears and repented of his sins against the Lord.

3:3   And the Lord told the prophet: "Come back from Ramath into the land of Judah, to the governor[11] of Moab, Maccabeus."

---

[10] This identification seems like the author might be speaking of the city of Rabat-Ammon, which, while still not in Moab, is on the correct side of the Jordan river.
[11] Here the word king is not used, rather that of a court official or leader. Perhaps in the context of Judas Maccabee, an ethnarch.

3:4	He said to him: "Tell him 'The Lord has spoken to you'. Tell him 'He said to you, I, the Lord, Who is your Creator, sent you by My will, so that you might destroy My nation.'
3:5	So that he might not say: 'I destroyed the dignity of the land of Jerusalem by the strength and the power of my hand, by the size of my army.'
3:6	For it is not you, [Maccabeus], that did this thing. [Israel] has made Me melancholy with all her avarice, treachery, and lasciviousness.
3:7	I have abandoned her and placed her under your authority, and now the Lord forgives you of your sins because of the birth of your children.
3:8	It is not for your sake, who sought strength in the power of your mind, and said 'I have laid siege to the land of Jerusalem by the strength of my authority.'
3:9	Have no doubt about this. For those who doubt are unable to enter into repentance. Truly, by the confines of your understanding you will enter into repentance.
3:10	Those men are extolled who enter into repentance without any doubts, and who never again return to their desire for sin, for they turned away because of their transgressions.
3:11	Men are praised who return to the Lord, their Creator, having been made strong through mourning and weeping, in prostration and supplication.
3:12	Men are extolled who conduct themselves rightly and enter into repentance as [the Lord] has commanded them.
3:12	'Those who come to repentance, you are my treasure, for you have turned away from your dishonesty to repent'."
3:13	[Rei] said these things to Maccabeus the arrogant when he returned to [the Lord] after losing his way and entering repentance.

3:14   "I have forgiven you of your sins because of your fear and terror, for I, the Lord, am your Creator, who places suffering on children because of the sins of the father up to the seventh generation[12], if the child commits the sin of the father.

3:15   For Who is the one who grants clemency for at least ten thousand generations for all those who love Me and keep My law?

3:16   Truly, I will fulfill My promise to you, because of these, your children, whom you have borne."

3:17   And the Lord, Who is sovereign over all, and Who granted dignity upon Israel, said: "I will accept your repentance in spite of the sin that you have made."

3:18   Thereafter, [Maccabeus] went out from the pit and prostrated himself before the prophet, saying, "Since I have angered the Lord, make of me what you will.

3:19   Let the Lord do this to me, so that I may not be separated from you, as we are lawless.

3:20   I did not live gracefully by His laws as did my fathers. For you know that we were taught by our fathers, and that still we worship the idols.

3:21   I am a sinner, who dwelled with my sins, who was locked in the grip of my own thoughts, and by the hubris of my rationality, I have offended the Lord's law.

3:22   Yet, until this moment, I had not heard the word of the prophets, the Lord's servants, and did not obey his law or those things which were asked of me."

3:23   He told me, saying: "Since there have been none of your kin before you, who believed their transgression, I knew that the prophet had welcomed on this day my repentance.

3:24   For now, abandon your worship of the idols, and return your mind to the Lord, that you might have true repentance," he said.

---

[12] This is the generational curse found elsewhere in the canonical scriptures Ex. 34:7

3:25	He knelt, bowing before the prophet's feet, to which the prophet lifted him up and ordered him to all those good works that he was due.
3:26	Therefore, he returned to his home and did all of the commands of the Lord.
3:27	Maccabeus then returned to the worship of the Lord, and he demolished the idols from his home. He removed all those who practiced witchcraft, idolatry, infidels, and magicians.
3:28	In the morning and evening, as their fathers had, he would teach the children that he brought captive from Jerusalem in the commands of the Lord, in His orders and His law.
3:29	From those captive children, he placed educated ones over his house.
3:30	From those infants, he appointed educated children, who tended to the youngest among them, who appeared before them and taught them the laws of the Lord, as the children of Israel learn.
3:31	He would hear from among the captive children of Israel the order, law, and the nine laws[13], and that the nation of Moab and their temples were all in vain.
3:32	[Maccabeus] destroyed their temples, their idols, priests, and their sacrifices. He destroyed the wine offering to the idols, morning and evening, as well as the goats and fatted lambs.
3:33	He destroyed his idols, whom he had worshiped in supplication, and believed all of their works, making sacrifices to them, day and night.
3:34	For all the priests requested this, as did his idols, from whom he served.
3:35	It had seemed to him that they offered salvation in all the things they spoke, but he did not doubt all those things said to him.
3:36	Maccabeus abandoned their worship, after he had heard the word of Rei, who was said to be a prophet.

---

[13] That is to say, the ten commandments.

3:37　He completed his work in repentance. Yet, the children of Israel would place sorrow in the Lord later and be chastised by Him in tribulation.

3:38　They knew this and cried to the Lord, all of his kin did right in the sight of the Lord, more than the children of Israel at that time.

3:39　At that time, he heard that [the children of Israel] were ensnared and abused at the hands of their enemies, and therefore they cried to [the Lord].

3:40　[The Lord] remembered their father's covenant and that time that they would be forgiven, for the sake of their fathers: Isaac, Abraham, and Jacob.

3:41　When [the Lord] did save them, they again forgot the Lord's salvation from tribulation, and they returned to their former ways of idolatry.

3:42　Again, He would rise against them people who would place punishment over them, and then make their tribulation known, who would inflict sorrow upon them, and they would cry to the Lord.

3:43　Yet, because of His love, and since they were the creation of His hand, He would grant them kindness and clemency.

3:44　In those days, He kept them until they again returned to their transgression, which offended [the Lord] because of the work of their hands, worshiping the idols in their assemblies.

3:45　He would rise against them the nations of Moab and Philistinia, Syria, Midian and Egypt, who then soundly defeated them, for which they would lament.

3:46　Those people would oppress them, taxing them and ruling over them. The Lord would then raise up princes for them, that at the proper time He might offer His salvation.

CHAPTER IV

4:1 In the days of Joshua, the Lord saved him.

4:2 And in the days of Gideon, again the Lord offered His salvation.

4:3 And in the days of Samson, and with Deborah and Barak, and in the days of Judith, was when the Lord came to save. Whether male or female, He would raise up a prince for them, who would spare them from the hands of their enemies, who sought to subjugate them.

4:4 For the love of God was given to save them from all those who sought to subjugate them.

4:5 They would rejoice in the works of the Lord, in all the deeds that He had done for them. They would rejoice in the harvest of their land, and in the multitude of their flocks and livestock in the wilderness.

4:6 [The Lord] would bless their fields and livestock, for He placed them into the eye of mercy, and He would not decrease the state of their livestock, for they are the children of kindness, and the beloved of [the Lord].

4:7 Yet, in those days, they were of wicked deed, and He would cast them into the hands of their enemies.

4:8 He would again destroy them, and they would seek to worship Him. They would return from their sin and march towards the Lord in repentance.

4:9 Then, they would return to their senses, and they would atone to the Lord for their sins. He would forget all those previous transgressions made against Him, for He knows them, that they are flesh and blood, and are fallible to moral thoughts within them, and those demons also within.

4:10 Yet, when Maccabeus heard this order that the Lord had made at His place of worship, the temple, he was slain in repentance.

SECOND BOOK OF ETHIOPIAN MACCABEES

4:11 When he had seen and heard this, he did not stop from doing righteous deeds that the children of Israel did when the Lord had forgiven them, after they had broken from the law and wept for the punishment of the Lord. For again, the Lord would forgive them, and they would keep His law.

4:12 Just the same, Maccabeus made straight his own deeds and kept His law; and he would abide closely by the commandments of the Lord, Israel's Creator.

4:13 Thereafter, he heard all of the deeds of boasting by the children of Israel, and he too would boast like them about keeping the law of the Lord.

4:14 He demanded that all of his kin and children abide closely in the commandments of the Lord in the fullness of His law.

4:15 He prohibited all those things that were prohibited in Israel, and he heard and kept the law that Israel kept. Despite his kin being from Moab, he also prohibited the food that is prohibited in Israel.

4:16 Moreover, he would offer tithes. He gave his firstborn, along with cattle, sheep, a donkey, and, returning to Jerusalem, offered sacrifices as Israel does.

4:17 He would absolve his sin and make sacrifices, one for the state of his past welfare, one for the present state, and one sacrifice for continuity.

4:18 He gave of his first crops, and poured out the wine that Israel poured out, giving it to the priests whom he had appointed. Likewise, he did all those things that Israel does and became sweet as incense.

4:19 [Maccabeus] built a tent with a candlestick, a bowl, a seat and four links of a ring[14]. He created oil for the lamps of the Holy of Holies, and the curtain that is made by Israel for the Holy of Holies when they served the Lord.

---

[14] See Ex. 25:12

4:20	They all did mighty deeds and abided closely to the order and law of the Lord. In those days the Lord did not neglect them or cast them into the hands of their enemies. Maccabeus did mighty deeds just as they did.
4:21	He would prostrate himself before the Lord, Israel's creator, every day, that [the Lord] might teach him, and that he might not become separate from the children of Israel, whom He chose, and who did His will.
4:22	Again, he would ask the Lord for a house in Jerusalem and children in Zion, that [the Lord] might give them the divine seed of virtue in Zion, and a Spiritual temple of the soul in Jerusalem, so that [the Lord] might save him from the wrath that the prophet spoke. He sought to accept his repentance by mourning and weeping before the Lord, expressing his sorrow and entering into repentance.
4:23	So that the Lord may not destroy the children of the world and that He might preserve him in his thoughts and deeds.
4:24	Those people from Moab, who abided below the authority of Maccabeus, rejoiced in the belief that their prince lived in righteous deeds. Therefore, they would regard his judgment and do his will. They would disregard the tongue of their nation and its justice, for they understood that Maccabeus' deeds excelled and were flawless.
4:25	They would all come and listen to the judgements of Maccabeus in truth and charity.
4:26	[Maccabeus] grew wealthy, having female and male slaves, camels and donkeys, and five hundred horses that wore breastplates. He would decimate the Amalekites and Philistines, and all those people of Syria. Formally, when he worshiped idols, they had defeated him.
4:27	He was victorious, for he worshiped the Lord before entering battle from that day forward and could not be defeated in battle.

SECOND BOOK OF ETHIOPIAN MACCABEES

4:28   Yet, they still came, by the power of their idols, to attempt to defeat him. They would call upon their idols' names and curse [Maccabeus], but no one could defeat him for his faith was in the Lord.

4:29   Therefore, after he had accomplished this, defeating his enemies, he lived and ruled his people by his authority.

4:30   He destroyed the unjust, and he would instill justice upon the orphans.

4:31   He would welcome widows in their destitution, feeding the hungry, and clothing the naked with his clothes.

4:32   And he would rejoice at the work of his hands, giving in the fullness of charity, granting his tithe to the temple. Maccabeus died thereafter, rejoicing to the end.

CHAPTER V

5:1   He died leaving his children still young. Still they grew up just as their father taught them. They kept the order of the household and their kin. They would care for the needs of the poor, of widows, and of orphans.

5:2   They would fear the Lord, granting alms to the poor, and they would keep the faith of their father. They would comfort the orphan in their destitution, acting as their adopted parents, protecting them from the hands of those who might have wronged them. They would calm them from all the distress and sorrow upon them.

5:3   They lived for five years while they did this.

5:4   Following this, the king of Chaldea[15], Tseerutsaydan, appeared. He destroyed all those in the nation, capturing the children of Maccabeus and destroying all their villages.

---

[15] The identification with Chaldea here appears to be intentional, pairing the tyrannical reign of Antiochus IV with that of Nebuchadnezzar II, both opponents to Jewish autonomy in antiquity.

5:5	He plundered all of their wealth, for they abided in their evil deeds and sin, in adultery, wickedness and greed, not remembering their creator. Therefore, those people who did not abide by the law of the Lord and His commands, and who worshiped idols, captured them and carried them away to their country.
5:6	He plundered their wealth, living highly upon their evil deeds and sin, with greed and adultery. They ignored the Lord their creator, and did as they pleased without the command of the Lord and His law. They captured those who worshiped idols and subdued their nation. They consumed the flesh of beasts and their blood[16], just as vultures consume a carcass. They accepted all those things that are forbidden by the Lord, for they had no structure from the commands of the Lord, as written in the law.
5:7	They did not know the Lord, their creator, who sent them forth from their mother's wombs and fed them those things they needed for the cure.
5:8	They married their aunts and their father's wife, and their stepmother[17], becoming criminals and pursuing evil things in sin and adultery. Yet, they had no sense of the time of judgment, for they committed all their evil deeds, such as marrying their aunts and their sisters, for they had no law.
5:9	For all their ways were dark and slippery, and their deeds were sinful and full of impropriety.
5:10	Those children of Maccabeus kept the order, refusing to eat unclean meat, which had been beaten and stored. They refused the deeds of the Chaldeans, for their works were evil and unrecorded in this book. Those were the deeds of sinners, apostates and criminals, infidels filled with thievery and and sin, as belonging to the children of pagans.

---

[16] This appears to be the dietary prohibition against consuming blood (Lev. 17:13-14).
[17] This is akin to the biblical prohibition on incest (Lev. 18:7-18; 20:11-21)

5:11 All the deeds that are good to their creator, the Lord, were unknown to them.
5:12 And they would again worship the idol, Belphegor[18], whom they would trust as if it were their creator, the Lord, as if they were deaf and dumb. For it is an idol, whom someone had worked, fashioned by a smith with silver and gold, that has no life or knowledge, and cannot see or hear.
5:13 It does not eat or drink.
5:14 It does not kill or save.
5:15 It does not plant or uproot.
5:16 It offers nothing to its friend or enemy.
5:17 It does not grant or remove honor.
5:18 It is a drain that misled the Chaldeans, who were lazy, for it does not give punishment or forgiveness.

CHAPTER VI

6:1 Tseerutsaydan, the enemy of the Lord, was arrogant and appointed priests for his idols, who disguise the falsehood.
6:2 He would make sacrifices for them and pour out wine for them.
6:3 It would seem to him that they ate and drank.
6:4 At sunrise he would offer them cows, donkeys, and heifers. He would make sacrifices morning and evening, and he would eat of his unclean sacrifices[19].
6:5 He would force those around him that they might also make sacrifices to the idols so that he would not be alone in this.

---

[18] From 'Baal Peor', "Lord of the Gap" who is mentioned in Num. 25:3
[19] This characterization seems to be largely analogous to that of the First Book of Ethiopian Maccabees. It therefore might be assumed that this author was already familiar with the text and its authority within the Ethiopian church.

SECOND BOOK OF ETHIOPIAN MACCABEES

6:6 At that time, they saw the children of Maccabeus, for they were handsome and they worshiped the Lord, their creator. The priests of the idols sought to mislead others, making sacrifices and eating from their unclean sacrifices. Yet, these honored children of Maccabeus refused to do so.

6:7 For they kept their father's command, and they were firm in their good deeds, for they feared the Lord and refused to agree.

6:8 And at that time they bound them and insulted and robbed them.

6:9 They informed the king, Tseerutsaydan, that they refused to sacrifice and bow before his idols.

6:10 The king, therefore, was disturbed, and he ordered that they might bring them forth. They were brought forth and stood before him, and the king said to them: "Make sacrifices to my idols".

6:11 They said to him: "We will not answer you in this matter, and will not make sacrifices to your defiled idols."

6:12 He frightened them with his many works, yet he could not make them, for they were disciplined in their belief in the Lord.

6:13 He set a fire and cast them into it, and they gave their bodies for the Lord.

6:14 After they died, they arose and were seen by him at night, with their swords drawn, when he was reclining upon his royal throne, and he was afraid.

6:15 "My lords, speak to me, what should I do for you? Do not take my body into death, that I might do all that you command me."

6:16 They told him that he is responsible for, saying: "Think that the Lord is your creator, and the Lord will send you away from this, your kingdom, where you have been arrogant. He will lower you into the fire of Gehenna with your father the devil. For we worship our Creator, the Lord, without a sinful life or wronging you. We bowed for Him in fear of His might, just as you burned us in the fire, you will complete all your tribulation just the same.

6:17 For [the Lord] who created all things, heaven and earth, the sea and everything that is within her,

6:18 and for Him that created the moon and the sun and stars—it is Him who made all of creation, the Lord.

6:19 For there is no other god in heaven or earth. He is the one who is sovereign over everyone, and there is nothing that is beyond Him. It is He who kills and saves, who whips in tribulation, and He who forgives. When we bow before Him in fear, just as you burned us in the fire, your punishment will be likewise." They said to him:

6:20 "Since He is the ruler of heaven and earth, and there is no one who escapes from His authority.

6:21 There is nothing that is in creation that He did not work, or can depart from His command apart from you, who are a criminal. For criminals act as you, who take their thoughts from their father, Satan, they hide. You and your priests and your idols will descend together into Gehenna, where there is no escape for all time.

6:22 Your teacher is Satan who taught you your evil deeds that you might commit evil upon us. Yet, it is not only you who commit this, and you all will descend into Gehenna forever.

6:23 For you make yourself like the Lord God, and forget that the Lord created you.

6:24 Your arrogance is present in your idols and in the work of your hands, until the Lord brings you low. He shall make his conviction on you because of all your iniquity and transgression that you have committed in this world."

CHAPTER VII

7:1 "Woe to you who do not know that the Lord created you, for your idols are in your image! For you have them, and might become regretful, for they will not benefit you when the time comes when you are thrown down into the constraints of the grave. Woe to you! For those among you who do keep His word and His law.

7:2 You will have no escape from this until the infinite age. You and your priest, who makes sacrifices for them as if they were the Lord God—your idols have no breath or soul, they do not offer revenge or destruction to those who do evil things to them, nor do they offer reward for good deeds.

7:3 Woe to you who sacrifice to them! For they are the work of human hands, the place where Satan lives, abiding there to mislead those lazy ones who think as you do. He seeks to lower you into the fire of Gehenna, with your priest who serves demons commanded for you and your idols.

7:4 For you do not understand that this will gain you nothing, for you live in error.

7:5 As for the animals that the Lord created to be food for you, as well as the dogs and beasts, they are better than you, for they die one death and have no other condemnation placed upon them.

7:6 Yet, you will die and receive punishment in the fires of Gehenna, where there is no escape for eternity. Animals fare better."

7:7 Having said this, they went away and hid from him.

7:8 That Tseerutsaydan remained and shook, consumed in fear, a fear that did not leave him until dawn.

CHAPTER VIII

8:1 He lived defiantly in maliciousness and arrogance.

8:2 And, as iron is said to be strong, as Daniel saw it upon his kingdom, he turned to the peoples of the nations within his kingdom.

8:3 He abided in his wickedness and his sloth, disturbing those around him.

8:4 He annihilated what we[20] previously said and he consumed other people's wealth.

8:5 For he steadfastly observed evil, like his father, the devil, who hardened his heart, and with his army, he destroyed what remained.

8:6 He said: "My time has become like that of the daylight", for he did not know that the Lord was his Creator.

8:7 In his heart, he thought that the sun was found within him.

8:8 He arose in strength. He camped in the place of the tribe of Zebulon, and began his recruitment in Macedonia. He received his rations from Samaria, and they gave him gifts there.

8:9 He made camp in the land of nomads, and went up into Sidon. He levied tax upon Greece, and elevated the desires of his heart as far as the flowing sea. Thereafter, he returned and sent his messengers as far as the Indian sea.

8:10 Just the same, he raised the thoughts of heart up into the heavens.

8:11 He lived strongly in his arrogance and evil, for he did not have any humility.

8:12 And he took the path towards darkness and slipperiness, towards criminality and arrogance, towards the shedding of blood and tribulation.

---

[20] This "we" is unclear.

8:13	He did all of those things that are abominable to the Lord. He did as his teacher did, the devil, who educated him in evil and transgression. He made the orphan weep and showed his cruelty to the poor.
8:14	He defeated and annihilated the kings of different peoples by his authority.
8:15	He reigned over the enemy chief and the many peoples. He taxed them as he pleased.
8:16	Even when he conquered, he did not stop. There was no man whom he did not ensnare, starting from the sea of Tarshish[21] and going to the sea of Jericho[22].
8:17	He would bow to idols, and would consume dead creatures with their blood, which a sword had cut and which had been sacrificed to idols. All his deeds were done without justice, for he had none. For he was one who frightened people with his authority, and levied taxes as he wished.
8:18	Because he did what he wished, there was no fear of the Lord in him. He abided in maliciousness before the Lord, his Creator.
8:19	He did not obey his Creator, for he did evil against his companions, who were frustrated and captured him. The Lord also granted him hardship.
8:20	And the Lord said: "I will destroy and take my vengeance on sinners who did not live by my commandments. No one will utter their names in this world." Just as he annihilated ancient peoples, [the Lord] shall cast His vengeance and destruction upon that at the proper time.
8:21	For just as the wicked do wicked things, they shall receive their rightful burden.
8:22	Yet, since it is commanded by the Lord, righteous deeds flow from people who commit to righteousness.

---

[21] Here meaning the Mediterranean Sea, but its broader biblica use is ambiguous (Ex. 28:20; 1 Ki. 10:22; Ps. 72:10)
[22] That is to say, the Dead Sea.

SECOND BOOK OF ETHIOPIAN MACCABEES

8:23 For Joshua destroyed in one day the five kings of Canaan[23], and made the sun stand in Gibeon by his prayer[24], so that he might destroy their armies. The sun stood there in the heavens until he destroyed the armies of the Hivites and Canaanites, Perizzites, Hittites, and Jebusites. He slew about twenty thousand of them at that time. He bound them foot to neck and slew them, killing them in a cave with his spear, covering them with stone.

8:24 Suffering like this will find all people who anger the Lord by their evil deeds.

CHAPTER IX

9:1 Oh weak man, you are not the Lord! Why are you so proud? You who are in plain sight on this day a man, will be the ashes of the earth tomorrow, and become worms in your grave.

9:2 For your teacher is the devil, who returns the evil works by all men towards themselves, just as he misled our father Adam.

9:3 Just as with him, Sheol will find you and find all those who work your sin.

9:4 [The devil] hardened his heart and made himself proud, refusing to bow to Adam, who was made by God.

9:5 You, by the same measure, have refused to bow before your Creator, the Lord, just as the devil did.

9:6 Like your fathers before you, who have no knowledge of the Lord their Creator and did not worship Him.

9:7 They will go to Gehenna[25], and you also.

---

[23] See Josh. 10:16-43
[24] See Josh. 10:13
[25] The regular use of 'Gehenna' here, as well as the Hebrew 'Sheol', are historical curiosites, as the author never utilizes the familiar Greek 'Hades' found elsewhere in the Greek Scriptures. Perhaps this is a point of differentiation, as Hades conveys the Amnesis of the soul, wherein Gehenna has no such connotation. Far more likely, the author composed this text in a period where Hellenic diction had fallen out of favor in Axumite and Nubian kingdoms.

9:8 And you have aroused His anger, for you have abandoned the worship of the Lord, Who gave you dominion over the five kingdoms. Does it seem to you that you will escape from the Lord's dominion?

9:9 You do act as you should, according to His will. He sees you, and if you commit righteous deeds in this world, the Lord will support you in your deeds. He will bless you and protect you, and all the deeds of your hands. He will subject your enemies, past and present, to your hand.

9:10 You will rejoice in all of your proceedings and goings forth, and in the child born of your nature, and in the fatness of your flocks, and in all the deeds which you commit by your hand, and in all the thoughts of your heart. For authority has been given to you by the Lord, that you might do as He wills—laboring, planting, and harvesting. All of this will be commanded for you.

9:11 Yet, if you will not listen to the word of the Lord, or live strongly in His law, you will be like the criminals who came before you. They are the men who do not worship the Lord as is demanded, and who do not believe strongly in the narrowness of His law. There is no place where you will be able to accept from the authority of the Lord, for the judgements of the Lord are true[26].

9:12 All is completely revealed to Him, and there is nothing hidden to Him.

9:13 He is the One who ensnares the kings' authority, and Who overturns the thrones of the powerful ones.

9:14 He is the One who raises up those who are weak, and He lifts up those who are lowly.

9:15 He is the One who loosens their bounds, and Who raises them from the dead. For the waters of absolution are near Him, and at the appointed time, He will raise those whom He loves, whose flesh is no more, and has decayed and become like the dust.

---

[26] See Ps. 19:9

9:16 After having cast judgment upon those who work evil deeds, He will take them down into Gehenna, for they have offended Him.

9:17 They have eliminated the order of the Lord and His law. He will annihilate their children from the earth.

9:18 For the deeds of the righteous are harder to perform than that of the sinners' works. Sinners do not wish to walk in the council of the righteous.

9:19 Just as the heavens are distant from the earth, likewise righteous peoples' deeds are distant from the deeds of the wicked.

9:20 The work of sinners is thievery, adultery, iniquity, avarice, and infidelity. They are drunk on their iniquity, robbing those around them of their money.

9:21 It is a lust for the shedding of blood, and lunging towards the path of self-destruction. It is the making of weeping orphans, and eating the blood of the flesh. It is eating the flesh of the camel and the boar. It is the defilement of a woman in her blood, and a woman in childbirth.

9:22 All of these are the deeds of a sinner. They are the entrapment of Satan, a wide and prepared path that takes all towards Gehnna to abide forever, and into Sheol.

9:23 Yet, the path of the righteous is very narrow, and it takes those towards humility, innocence, oneness, love, prayer, fasting, life, and the purity of the flesh. It keeps those away from what is pernicious, from eating what was cut by a sword, and what was left to rot, and from approaching the wife of a youth and adultery.

9:24 They stay away from what was not commanded by the law, from eating illicit food and the acts of hatred. They avoid the works that offend the Lord, for only the sinners do this.

9:25 As for the righteous, they distance them from all the acts that are offensive to the Lord.

9:26 He loves them and will keep them from all suffering, guarding them as His wealth.

9:27	For they keep His order and His law, and all those things that He loves, yet Satan is sovereign over sinners.

CHAPTER X

10:1	Fear the Lord who created you and has kept you up until this day. All you nobles and kings, do not go upon the path of Satan.
10:2	Live in the law and command of the Lord, who is sovereign; do not go upon the path of Satan.
10:3	At one time, the children of Israel fought against Amalek, so that they might come to proprietorship of the lands of the Hitties, Canaanites, and Perizzites. As Balak son of Zippor said to Balaam[27]:
10:4	"Those whom you curse will be cursed, and those whom you bless will be blessed. Do not go down the road of Satan, for I will give you an allotment of silver and gold to honor you, so that you might curse for me. And having cursed, that you might destroy for my part."
10:5	For this Balaam made his sorcery a lesson, and Balak son of Zippor showed him the place where the children of Israel were encamped.
10:6	He had stated his doubts and made his sacrifice, having slaughtered the fattened calves and sheep. For he wished to curse and destroy the children of Israel.
10:7	[The Lord] returned his curse as a blessing. Yet, the Lord did not wish to curse them by His word, as to not go down Satan's road.
10:8	"Since you are the kin of those the Lord has chosen, and are the abode of the Lord from heaven, let those who curse you be cursed. I will make all those who bless you be blessed," He said.
10:9	And at that time he blessed them before him, and Balak son of Zippor was saddened, being upset that he did not curse them as commanded.

---

[27] This episode appears in Numbers 22-24

10:10 For the king of the Lord that has been blessed has come into this country, and Balaam said to him: "I will not curse Israel, whom the Lord has blessed."

10:11 Balak, son of Zippor, said to Balaam: "As for me, I wished that you might have cursed me. You blessed them before me and did not curse them. If you had cursed them for me and said 'give this to me', I would have given you a house filled with silver and gold; instead you blessed them. You did not do right by me and I will not do right by you."

10:12 Balaam said, "What the Lord told me to speak with my tongue, I will speak. Yet, as for me, I cannot ignore something brought by the Lord.

10:13 If I curse the blessed kin, the Lord will be displeased by my love of money. As for me, I do not love money more than I do my soul.

10:14 As the Lord said to their father Jacob, 'Let those who bless you be blessed, and let those who curse you be cursed.' Therefore, I cannot curse the blessed Jacob. I do not love money more than that of my soul." He said, and the Lord has said:

10:15 "Let those who bless you be blessed, and let those who curse you be cursed." Finish your work and your path so that the Lord might love it.

10:16 Do not be like those former people, who offend the Lord with their sin, and whom He has neglected. For they are those who have been destroyed in the waters of destruction.

10:17 There are also those whom He destroyed by the hands of their enemies, and those whom He destroyed by those who hate them, and brought the evil of their enemies upon them in tribulation. They captured their chief men, their priests, and prophets.

10:18 They were delivered to a foreign nation that they were alien to. They were captives and were plundered of their livestock, and destruction fell upon them and their nation.

10:19 They have destroyed the honor of Jerusalem, its lands, its walls and ramparts, and leveled Jerusalem into a field.

10:20 The priests were taken captive, and the law was destroyed. The warriors fought and fell in battle.

10:21 And the widows were captured. When they were taken, they wept for their fate, yet they did not weep for their dead husbands.

10:22 The children wept, and the elders were ashamed. They were unkind to both the elders and those with gray hairs.

10:23 They slew all those that were found in the country. They were cruel to the beautiful ones and those who observed the law. For the Lord has been angered against His people at that time, and wished to demolish His home, the Temple. They captured it and took them as captives to an alien land and alien peoples.

10:24 God was grieved by this again, because of those times when the Lord neglected the children of Israel. The Lord made Jerusalem to be plowed like a field[28].

10:25 Yet, He showed His kindness for their fathers' sake, that He did not destroy them at that time. For [the Lord] loved their fathers, Abraham, Isaac and Jacob, who abided in truth and lived disciplined in the law before their creator. It was for the sake of their fathers, and not for their own sake, that the Lord forgave them.

10:26 He appointed them to honors that were in confluence, giving them two kingdoms, one upon the earth and one in heaven.

10:27 Upon the kings and princes who dwell in this temporal world, just as your fathers lived disciplined in the deeds that were expected of them in the past, and they therefore inherited the kingdom of heaven. Remember them, and be like them, for their names are beatified by their children's children.

10:28 And you, make straight your deeds, that [the Lord] might straighten up your kingdom for your sake; so that your name might be called blessed, and named like the just monarchs who went before you, who served the Lord in their beatific ways.

---

[28] See Mic. 3:12

CHAPTER XI

11:1   Remember the Lord's servant, Moses, who was not consternated when he dwelt amongst his kin in humility[29], for he prayed so that they might be spared, pleading with the Lord for the innocence of his brothers and sisters who betrayed him. He loved the Lord, and sought that he would not destroy them. He said, "Since they have wronged you, Lord, forgive and do not abandon your people". And he, therefore, atoned for their sins. So, remember Moses, the servant of the Lord, and his lack of consternation.

11:2   "For I have wronged You, forgive Your servant, a sinner, for You are merciful. You are the pardoner and forgiver of my sins."

11:3   Moses likewise atoned for the sin of his brother and sister, who betrayed him[30].

11:4   And because of this, [Moses] was called innocent.

11:5   The Lord loved him more than all the children of the priest[31], who were his brethren. For [the Lord] appointed priests. He made [Moses] holy like His own majesty.

11:6   He, therefore, sank into the earth like the children of Korah, who were bold. He had them lowered into Sheol with their livestock and their tents, and they said "we are here, in flesh and in spirit". For as the Lord God has loved him, and did not depart from His commands, all that was spoken was done for him just as the word of the Lord.

11:7   Unless you have destroyed the command of the Lord, He will do you accordingly, and will keep the kingdom for you.

11:8   Asaph's and Korah's children[32], who departed from Moses' law, complained to him, because he spoke "straight your hearts to be ruled by the Lord".

---

[29] See Num. 12:3
[30] See Num. 12:1
[31] See Num. 3:10
[32] This appears to be an allusion to the revolt led by the sons of Korah. However, in the biblical account they do not die (Num. 26:11).

11:9 They complained, saying "Are we not sons of Levi, who perform the work of priests in the tabernacle?"

11:10 They went, therefore, burning incense, grasping their censers as they did so. Yet, the Lord did not accept this, and they were burnt by the fire of their censers, which melted them like wax in the heat of the fire. And no one remained from among them, as the Lord spoke: "Their censers were honored by their burnt flesh". Of those who entered into the Lord's house without His command, neither their clothes, nor their bones will remain.

11:11 Thereafter, the Lord said to Aaron and Moses: "Gather those censers into the tabernacle. Let it be an instrument for my house, wherein I made all things, inside and out."

11:12 And he prepared this honor for the instruments of the tabernacle. [Aaron] prepared the rings and the joiners, and the sea of the pictures of angels[33].

11:13 He made the cups, the curtains, the grounds of the tabernacle, the altar and the jugs, wherein they made sacrifices reserved only for the tabernacle.

11:14 They made their sacrifices by their own hands, sacrifices for their sustenance, sacrifices for the atonement of sins, and the vow of a sacrifice, performed night and day.

11:15 All this He asked of Moses, to perform in the tabernacle of the Lord, that they might please Him with their deeds.

11:16 They did not curse because of the rule of the Lord God, that His name might be praised in the law, and in the tabernacle of the Lord. He gave them a promise that they might come to inherit the land of milk and honey that he pledged to their father Abraham.

11:17 They did not curse the rule of the Lord God, who had promised Isaac, and continued to worship with Jacob,

11:18 who continued this worship with Aran and Moses in the tabernacle,

---

[33] Presumably the author is alluding to the molten sea, although it is not described as such elsewhere (1 Ki. 7:23-26; 2 Chr. 42-5).

11:19 who continued this worship with Elijah and Samuel, and in the Temple of Solomon, who made it the house of the Lord in Jerusalem, and when the name of the Lord rested in the honor of Israel.

11:20 For [Jerusalem] is a supplication, and atonement of sins, which is made for those who abide in innocence and for the priests.

11:21 For she is a place for those who do His will, where He will hear their prayers,

11:22 and the foundation of the law of the Lord that honors Israel.

11:23 For she is where sacrifices are made, and where incense is burnt, that the Lord that honors Israel be of good smell.

11:24 The Lord would speak upon the joiner, where He grants forgiveness in the tabernacle. The light of the Lord would be revealed to Jacob's children, whom He has chosen as His beloved to abide in His law and His command.

11:25 Yet, those who ignored the law of the Lord will be like the children of Korah, who sank into the Earth. Just the same, sinners might enter towards Gehenna, which has no exits for all eternity.

CHAPTER XII

12:1 You who did not keep the law, that was commanded of you in the tabernacle, woe to you! Princes of Israel who did not do His will, but have done your own, you are arrogant and prideful, greedy and adulterous, filled with drunkenness and lies.

12:2 Now, since these things anger me, like chaff that is thrown into the fire to burn, like conflagrations that scorch the mountains, and like a cyclone that spills chaff from its place and casts it upon the earth and up towards heaven, I will place my wrath upon you.

12:3 The Lord, who cast honor on Israel, said: "I will therefore destroy all those who live in sin." Remember the Lord, who is sovereign over the earth, and is almighty.

12:4 He loves those who love Him, and those people who abide in His command. He will wash away their iniquity and their sins. [Therefore], do not be hard of heart and incredulous.

12:5 Make your mind straight for the sovereignty of the Lord, and place your trust in Him, that you might protect yourselves. [The Lord] shall save you from the hands of your enemies on your day of darkness.

12:6 In the hour of your please, I will tell you, "Behold, I am there with you in spirit. I will save you from your enemies' hand, for you have had faith in Me, and you have done as I commanded. You did not depart from My law, as your heart has been with My own." The Lord who reigns said, "I will not neglect you on that day of your need."

12:7 He loves all those that love Him, for He is the granter of clemency, full of kindness, and He preserves those who keep His law as His great wealth.

12:8 He has turned back His anger from them many times, for He knows that they are but flesh and blood, and therefore He pardons them. He does not destroy all those in His chastisement, or when those souls are separated from their flesh. They will return to the earth.

12:9 For He has created them, bringing them from darkness into life. They will not know the place where they abide, until that time the Lord elects that they might be brought forth from death into life. He will again separate their souls from their flesh, and earth will return to earth.

12:10 His will will bring them forth from death into life.

12:11 Yet, Tseerutsaydan denied the Lord, exceeding his conceit before the Lord. He made himself glorified for many days after abandoning Him.

12:12 "My time will become like those above, for it is I who send forth the sun, and I will never feel death," He said.

SECOND BOOK OF ETHIOPIAN MACCABEES

12:13 Before he finished speaking, the angel of death, whose name was Thilimyakos[34], rose and struck him in the heart, and he died in that manner, for he did not praise the Creator. He was removed from his beautiful life, only to perish because of his own exceeding arrogance, and his deeds of evil.

12:14 When the army of the King of Chaldea had camped in the city and squares of the country ready for a fight, they proceeded to destroy all of the country upon the time of his death. They plundered his livestock, and they did not spare the ministers who dwelt on the city's walls.

12:15 They sought to steal his money, and they took a small amount with them, and they cast fire upon his nation and returned to their own land.

CHAPTER XIII

13:1 These five children of Macabeus, who refused to eat the sacrifice of an idol, prepared their bodies for death.

13:2 For they knew that they cannot deceive the Lord, as they can with men. For the Lord's anger is greater than the anger of the king.

13:3 Therefore, knowing that this world will dissolve, and that the creation of the Lord will not reside forever, they gave their bodies to the flames so that they might be preserved from the flames to come.

13:4 For they knew that they would enter paradise one day, which would be more splendid than any epoch upon the earth. They would find the grace of the Lord better than in any time, so they gave their bodies to the fire.

---

[34] This name does not appear to be Ge'ez or Hebrew. Its origins are unclear, but most likely it is a transliteration of the Greek name 'Telemachus'. This name is not associated with the name of the angel of death in any Abrahamic tradition. Its insertion here is *sui generis*. It is possible that it is a confabulation of the name 'Temeluchus' which appears as the name of the devil in the apocryphal work the Apocalypse of Paul.

SECOND BOOK OF ETHIOPIAN MACCABEES

13:5   What is the eternal age? It is like that of a shadow, a small kernel of wax melting on the edge of the fire. Is it not like this?

13:6   Yet, You Lord abide forever, and Your time is never fulfilled. Your name will be called by children's children.

13:7   The children of Maccabeus had seen all of this, and refused to eat the illicit sacrifice, instead putting faith in the Lord.

13:8   They knew that they would rise with the dead, and, for the Lord's sake, knowing that they would see His judgment council after the resurrection, for this they gave their body to martyrdom.

13:9   And those people who do not know that the dead will rise, or have any faith, you will see later life that surpasses this earthly life. Beautification shall come, rising out of the five children of Maccabeus, who gave their bodies as one to the death because they knew the resurrection.

13:10   They believed in Him, knowing that all things pass. For this they did not bow to the idols, or eat of the illicit sacrifice that gives no favor. They gave their bodies over to death that they might gain the favor of the Lord.

13:11   Consequently, with the knowledge that He will make things new in flesh and spirit in the time to come, they showed no knowledge of this world's favor and the pain of death. This is a thing of seriousness to those with wives and children. Still they knew that the resurrection of the flesh and spirit would come upon the day of Advent[35], therefore, they gave their bodies to death.

---

[35] The appearance of this word is very specific as it is derived directly from the liturgical Latin- 'Adventus Christi'. That is to say, the coming of Christ, in this incidence the Christian eschatological hope of his second coming Christ at the end of time. Ergo, this text could not belong to the Beta Israel community as it is a unique adaptation of Catholic lexicon. This minor reference does grant some potential timeframe for its composition, as an Ethiopian delegation attended the Catholic Council of Florence in the middle of the 15th century.

SECOND BOOK OF ETHIOPIAN MACCABEES

13:12   They knew that those who keep the Lord's law, along with the princes and kings who trust the word of the Lord and were righteous,

13:13   they shall reign for their children's children for many years in the kingdom of heaven, where there is no sadness, or pain, or death. They shall know in their hearts what will be done at that time, just as wax melts before the fire. For this, they gave their bodies over to death.

13:14   They believed that their faces would shine sevenfold[36] more brightly than the sun. Therefore, they would rejoice in the love [of the Lord] at the time when they arose, body and soul, they gave their bodies over to death.

CHAPTER XIV

14:1   Yet, among the Samaritans and Jews, are the Sadducees, who do not believe in the resurrection of the dead. And also, the Pharisees, who make me[37] melancholy, and it helps me in my heart. "We die tomorrow," the Jews say. "Let us eat and drink, for tomorrow we die[38]. There will be no rejoicing when we see the grave."

14:2   The Samaritans too say, "Since our flesh is dust, it will not arise."[39]

14:3   Yet, since [the soul] is invisible like that of the wind, like that of the voice of thunder– behold, she is here! She is what can never be invoked, unseen as a soul that cannot arise when the flesh dies. We will have faith in our souls rising when the resurrection has come.

---

[36] See Is. 30:26
[37] Who is speaking here is unclear, as there is no clear reference before or after.
[38] See Is. 22:13, Prov. 23:35
[39] See Gen. 3:19

14:4 As beasts will eat [the flesh], and worms will consume it in the grave, our flesh will become likewise. It will turn to dust and ashes.

14:5 Those beasts who consumed will too become dust, and become like the grass. They have turned to dust, as if they were never created at all. They will disappear without a trace, and their flesh will never arise.

14:6 And the Pharisees say, "We believe that all those who have died and risen, will come and unite the souls with another flesh that is in heaven, and not upon the earth, where it can be destroyed and rotten flesh can be found."

14:7 The Saducees say, "After the soul leaves the flesh, we will not arise from those persons who have died. For the flesh and the soul cannot arise after death, and after we die we will not arise."

14:8 Since they err, and speak insultingly about the sovereignty of the Lord, they sadden Him.

14:9 They did not believe the Lord who had honored them. They have no hope for salvation. Even still, they have no hope that the dead might arise and be saved.

14:10 O Jews, who are blind in your heart, you are whom He created, being brought forth from nothingness to life. You are scorned as spittle, will you be ignorant to the Lord who has made you? Will the Lord, who created you in his image and in his example, fail in binding your flesh and spirit?

14:11 Since you cannot escape from the Lord's authority, do not attempt to convince yourself as such. You will arise, without your desire for it. For your suffering you will receive in Sheol, where you were taken to upon the time of your death. There will be a loveless judgment cast upon you.

14:12 The sin that is found in demons, they will place it in your mind, working it within you after you are born from your mother's womb, and will commit to it fervently as you come of age.

14:13 They will place [sin] within your body at the time of your death, and it will bring judgment upon those times they committed to wickness.

14:14 Just the same, there is sin in the hardness of their heart, as there are those who commit and are taken by sin. Its kin will exhibit more demons.

14:15 All of the souls of sinners will come from the edge of heaven, where they originate. Yet, their sin will bring them towards Gehenna, pulling them and bringing their soul from where they were.

14:16 After their flesh abides separately from their soul, the dew of the Lord's charity will rise, and they will be sevenfold like the flesh of their father Adam.

14:17 You who live in the grave also make errors. You make it seem that you only mislead others, you say, "The resurrection of the dead is not here," that they might depart from the command of the Lord in error.

14:18 He will raise you up and give you your judgment for all the deeds that you have done. Who shall avoid this, and remain as dust?

14:19 At that time, whether wines be your nature, or water be your nature, or Earth be your nature, or fire be your nature, it shall come.

14:20 And if a soul resided in you, having abided in Sheol, it shall come.

14:21 Those souls of the righteous will live in paradise and they shall rejoice.

14:22 But you– Judeans, Samaritans, Pharisees, and Samaritans, will abide in Sheol up until the time of your own judgment.

14:23 At that time you will see that the Lord will return your punishment for your sins because you have misled men.

14:24 "Those who died will not arise. Since death is coming, let us eat and drink." Since you have sat in the chair of Moses, and deceived others with those words, saying, "Those who died will not arise." You will see [the Lord] shall pay you your punishment.

14:25 Without knowing the Books of Torah[40], when you teach others the words of the books, you teach them in error. It would have been better if you had no learning, than to have such deceit.

14:26 It would have been better if you did not know the words of the books, when you propagate evil teaching to the Lord's children by your empty words.

14:27 For the Lord shows no favor having seen [your] countenance. For He will grant grace and glory, prepared for His beloved, those people who teach righteous deeds. Yet, you have already received your reward, from those things you have spoken and the deeds done.

14:28 There is nothing that you will escape from the Lord's authority, who will cast judgment upon you. He will repay you for your deeds, and for those who you taught, you will receive your sentence together.

14:29 Know this, that those who died will arise, and if they are among those who kept His law, they too will arise. Just as the earth sends forth its grass after the rains, He will command them to come forth from the grave, so that it is impossible for them to remain decaying and rotten.

14:30 Just as the living wood drinks the dew and sends forth leaves, at that time He appeases the earth with the rains. Just as wheat bears its grain, and just as its grain produces buds, it will be impossible for the earth to withhold her fruit from the Lord, if He desires it.

---

[40] Here the specific word 'torah' (ቶራህ) is used, and not just the ambiguous word for 'the law'.

14:31 And just as it is impossible for a woman who conceived to prevent her womb from opening upon the time of labor, it will be impossible for her to escape without giving birth.

14:32 As the dew has directed her towards the commands of the Lord, at that time she will bring them forth, one at a time after hearing the word of the Lord. The grave can also not prevent those from their resurrection.

14:33 All the flesh will be gathered together where the corpses have fallen. At that place the life of their souls will be opened, and the souls will return to the flesh from which they had been separated.

14:34 When the drums are beaten, those people who have died will quickly arise like that of the blinking of an eye. They will arise and stand before the Lord, and He will give them the reward of the work of their hands.

14:35 On that hour you will see that you have arisen with the dead, and you will stand in astonishment for all the deeds of your hand in this world. You will see all your sins composed before you, and will be filled with regret.

14:36 You know that you will arise with those who have died, and you will receive judgment as compensation for the deeds you have done.

CHAPTER XV

15:1 Those people who find their reward from their righteous deeds will rejoice at that hour. Yet, those who ignored this, saying "those who died will not arise," will be melancholy when they see at that time that the dead arose, and that their wicked deeds did not benefit them.

15:2 That their deeds will convict them, and they themselves will know that they are accountable, for there is no one alive who will be able to advocate for them.

15:3 When the day of judgment and weeping has come, when the Lord will come, and absolute judgments are passed, those people who forget the law of the Lord will be found in the place they stand.

15:4 On that day there will be complete darkness, and when the fog has lifted, when lightning flashes and thunder is heard,

15:5 when the earth shakes, and terror, and heat, and freezing rain all come,

15:6 the wicked who commit evil will receive their punishment. On that day an undefiled person will receive his reward because of the cleanliness of their hand, and all those who forget the law of the Lord will receive their punishment, just as sinners commit their sin, and they will stand in the place they are found.

15:7 On that day, the masters and mistresses will sit below their slaves in rank.

15:8 On that day, the kings will have the same dignity as the poor, the old will be treated as the young, mothers and fathers will be on equality with their child.

15:9 On that day, the rich will be the same as the poor, the arrogant will be the same as the lowly, the great will be the same as the meek. These will come on the day of judgment. For it is the day that sentence will be passed for punishment, and it is the day when all will receive what is due to them for the sin of their hand.

15:10 For that is the day when those who were righteous in deed will receive their reward, and those that committed wickedness will receive their punishment.

15:11 For that is the day when those who find their reward will rejoice, and those who have forgotten the law will stand there in their place. Those liars, who digest books and say "We will not rise again," will see the resurrection.

15:12 Then, all the sinners of the world, who ignore righteous deeds in this world, will weep because of the sin that they have worked, and sadness will fall on them without relief.

15:13 Just the same, the righteous who work deeds of kindness, they will rejoice and will not be satiated for all ages. For they have done what is right when they were in this world.

15:14 They have known that they will rise again after death, and they did not become alien to the law of their Creator.

15:15 Since they did not depart from His law, they will inherit two states, that [the Lord] will increase their descendents in this world, and that He will grant dignity upon those descendents.

15:16 He will grant to them the kingdom of Heaven, where they will find the comfort that was promised to their fathers at the time the dead arise, while those who were rich become poor.

15:17 Those who committed sin will weep, as well as those who are apostate to the resurrection, and who do not keep the law of the Lord, and do not think of the day of the resurrection.

15:18 On that day, they will see the tribulations coming to them, and which have no end, where there is no peace or calm, for they have only sadness, and no peace of mind.

15:19 [They will find] the fire that cannot be extinguished, and the worms that never sleep. This will find them.

15:20 In the place, they will be flesh [again] with fire, sulfur, cyclones, frost, hail and sleet, and all of this will rain upon them.

15:21 Those who do not believe the dead will live again, they will have the fire of Gehenna upon them.

CHAPTER XVI

16:1 You, please think upon your flesh, your feet and hands and nails, the hair upon your head, for the time comes soon when it will be cut. Have knowledge in the awakening by this token, that you have a mind, and that you have discipline and knowledge.

SECOND BOOK OF ETHIOPIAN MACCABEES

16:2 Your feet, hands and nails, and the hair upon your head, you say "where do it come from?" Is it not the Lord who prepared things so that they might proceed forth? [Just the same], do you know that the resurrection will happen to your flesh, that you might know that you will rise again after death?

16:3 Since you deceive others, while you say "There is no resurrection of the dead," on that day when the dead arise you will receive your punishment like those who committed sins of iniquity.

16:4 For even what you plant now will not refuse to grow, whether it be wheat or barley, you will see it upon the day and time when you receive your punishment.

16:5 Again, that which has been planted will not say "I will not grow", whether it is figwood or a grapevine, its fruit and leaves will not be changed.

16:6 If you plant grapes, it will never become a fig; and if you plant figs, it will not be transformed into that of grapes; and if you sow wheat, it will not become barley.

16:7 In every seed, there is its own kind, each of them fruits, each of them woods, each of them leaves and roots. Bring forth the fruit after the water of baptism and its benediction, for this comes from the Lord. Yet, if you sow barley, know therefore, that it will not be transformed into wheat.

16:8 Just the same, a grave might produce flesh and a soul. [The grave] will produce those who are like the Lord, for they have been sowed upon her. The flesh and the soul that the Lord sowed will rise again and be united. Those people who were righteous will not be transformed into the wicked, and the wicked will not become the righteous.

SECOND BOOK OF ETHIOPIAN MACCABEES

16:9 When hour has come that a drum is beaten, and all those who died will arise, upon the water of baptism from the Lord, those who work righteous deeds will arise to life in the resurrection. Their reward is rejoicing in the garden which God prepared for the good-hearted. There will be no pain or sickness, and that is the dwelling place of the clean ones, where they will live eternally.

16:10 Yet, all those who did evil deeds will arise to the final judgment, and with the devil who misled them,

16:11 and with his armies, the demons who deny any man be saved from among the sons of Adam.

16:12 They will descend down into Gehenna into the edge of darkness, where there is weeping and grinding of teeth[41]. In that place there is no charity or pardon, and no exits for all eternity, beneath in Sheol forever. For they did not work righteous deeds in their life in this world when they abided in the flesh.

16:13 For this thing, it will be judged against them, when flesh and soul are again united.

16:14 Woe to such men, who do not believe that the flesh and soul arise, when the Lord shows His great miracles at once.

16:15 All of them will receive their reward paid forward from the work of their tired hands.

CHAPTER XVII

17:1 A kernel of wheat will grow, or bear fruit, unless it first dies[42]. Yet, if a wheat kernel dies, it will send its roots upon the earth, and will send forth leaves, and buds, and it will bear fruit.

17:2 And you know that the single kernel of wheat will become many.

17:3 Just the same, this kernel will again rise from water, spirit, and the dew of the earth, for wheat cannot bear its harvest without the sun, which is the fixed place of fire.

---

[41] See Matt. 13:42
[42] See John 12:24

17:4 Also, the spirit, which is the fixed place of the soul. Because of this, wheat can bear its harvest without wind, and the earth gives water to drink, and satiate it.

17:5 After the earth, which is ashes, drinks of the water, she grows roots and grows forth upwards, and her harvest as much as the Lord has blessed her.

17:6 A wheat kernel is, therefore, an example of Adam, in whom there was an everlasting soul, placed there by the Lord. And likewise, a vine drinks water and send forth its roots, and its deep roots draw upon those waters.

17:7 The waters of baptism are from the Lord, and give drink to the long tendrils of the vines, which draw the waters upwards to its leaves. By the heat of the sun its buds upward, and by the will of the Lord, it bears its fruit.

17:8 It will be a lovely perfume that gives reason for rejoicing, and when they eat of it, it will satisfy them like water that will never make them thirst[43], and grains that never make them hungry. On that day, they will be filled with it, it will be their life blood.

17:9 As it is written in the Psalms: "wine makes a man's heart rejoice."[44] On that day, they will drink it, and it will make their hearts rejoice. Their mouths will be open and loose on that day, and they will be drunk. He will drink and fill his body with it, and the blood will flow towards his heart.

17:10 For as the wine of drunkenness misleads him, and deprives him of his reason, it will make pits and cliffs like a spacious meadow, and he will not know any stumbling blocks or thorns upon his feet or hands.

17:11 The Lord did as such upon the fruits and upon the vine, so that His name might be praised by all those who believe in the resurrection of the dead and do His will.

17:12 In the kingdom of heaven, [the Lord] will make all those rejoice in the resurrection.

---

[43] See John 4:13-14
[44] See Ps. 4:7

CHAPTER XVIII

18:1 You who do not believe in the resurrection of the dead, what error you live with! On that day, they will take you forward into a place that you do not know. You will have but futile regrets for you did not have faith in the rising of the dead, and the union of soul with flesh. On that day, you will be thrown into Gehenna.

18:2 Whether you do good or evil, you will receive the reward for your deeds. For those who have misled their companions' hearts, saying, "We know that the dead are dust and ashes, and will not arise."

18:3 For their death has no end, and they have no power over the chastisement that comes upon them. For they were not strong against their misfortune, and therefore, they misled their companions, who must stand before the court of the Lord.

18:4 On that day, [the Lord] was angry with them in His wrath, and they were afraid. For they did not know they were created out of emptiness into the light of being. For they speak the law of the Lord without knowing. This will be judged against them because of their wickedness.

18:5 They do not know Gehenna, where they will do, for they were conceited and dishonest in their deeds. They taught their companions to have a hungry heart, for they are wicked, teaching a wicked thing, saying "there is no resurrection of the dead".

18:6 On that day, they will know that the dead will arise again, and they will know that judgment will be cast upon them because of their doubt in the resurrection of all of Adam's children.

18:7 For all mankind are the children of Adam, and as such they have died because of Adam. Therefore, death and judgment will find them because of the transgression of Adam against the Lord.

18:8 They will rise again with their father Adam, so that they might receive recompense for their deeds, as death to rule over them because of the ignorance of Adam, their father.

18:9 Since the Lord's command was ignored by Adam they have received hardship, and their flesh will melt like wax in the grave, and their bodies will expire.

18:10 The earth will drink their marrow. They will perish and their beauty will vanish in the grave. Their flesh will be placed in the grave, and their eloquence will be buried under the earth.

18:11 Worms will proceed from their bright eyes, and their features will vanish in the grave and they will become dust.

18:12 Where is your beauty? You who were lovely, whose continence was fair and whose eloquence was graceful? Where is the strength of your warriors?

18:13 Where is the army of kings? Or that of your lords? Where is the decoration or your horses, in silver and gold, adorning your gleaming weapons. Did it not perish?

18:14 Where is the sweet wine, and the sumptuous food?

CHAPTER XIX

19:1 Let the earth gather its nobles and kings, its wealthy ones, its elders and its beautiful daughters, for misery has arisen from you.

19:2 O Earth, you who gathered those who were once warriors, those who were beautiful, and those who were of fine dress, all those full of knowledge, and those whose words were sweet eloquence like that of a harp, or lyre or violin.

19:3 All those who make music and rejoice with wine, and all those whose eyes shine like that of the morning star,[45]

19:4 and those who write down what is certain with their right hand lifted up, giving and taking as they have, and those whose feet were swift, and those who run like swift wheels. Woe when you arise.

---

[45] That is to say Venus, although in this case it might also be an allusion to Nebuchadnezzar in the book of Isaiah.

19:5 Oh death, which separates beautiful souls from their flesh, you have been sent by the will of the Lord so that we might arise from you.

19:6 Since you have gathered people which the Lord has made, and returned them to Him, you earth, they will arise from you, since we were found from you. They all have returned by the will of the Lord, and we were joyful because of the will of the Lord.

19:7 You, [earth], have become a carpet for our bodies. We return to you and we are buried within you. We ate of your fruit and you ate of our flesh.

19:8 We have drunk the waters found within your springs, and you have drunk of the springs of our blood. We ate of the fruit of the earth and you have eaten of the flesh of our bodies.

19:9 Just as the Lord has commanded you to be our sustenance, we are the grains of the earth filled with nourishment, and you have received the beauty of our flesh, making it into dust for your nourishment as the Lord has commanded.

19:10 Oh death, who has gathered the kings and nobles and all the mighty ones! Woe those who will arise, and did not fear the power and might belonging to the Lord, who created them and has commanded them. Oh death, woe to those who arise in scorning and suffering.

19:11 You were unkind to the righteous, and you did not take on the strong as warriors. You did not depart from the poor or the rich, nor the righteous or the wicked, nor children or elders, or women or men.

19:12 You did not depart from all those who are of pure thoughts and who did not violate the law, and you did not depart from those who were like beasts in their work, to whom think evil things, and were beatified in their features, actions, and word. Oh death, woe arising from you.

19:13 You did not depart from those whose words were angry, and whose mouths were full of conceit. You gathered those who live in darkness, and not in light of your place. Oh death, woe arising from you.

19:14 The earth gathered the flesh of those people who live upon the plain or in the caves, at the time when the drum is struck and all the dead arise.

19:15 As all people who have died will arise again, just as the wink of an eye by the command of the Lord, upon the striking of a drum. The wicked will receive their punishment for their sins in great abundance, just as the righteous who did good will rejoice.

CHAPTER XX

20:1 Believe me that all of the deeds committed in this world will not remain obscured on the day we stand before [the Lord] in fear and trembling[46].

20:2 On that day, we will not gather provisions from the path. On that day, we will not have clothes to adorn our bodies.

20:3 On that day, we will not have a staff to grasp or shoes on our feet.

20:4 On that day, we will not know the road which the demons take us, if it be smooth or slick, or if it be dark, or if it be thorny, or if it be filled with deep waters. Believe me that the deeds we commit in this world will not remain hidden.

20:5 They will not know the demons who take them, and not hear a thing.

20:6 They are the black ones, and they lead us into darkness, never exposing their faces.

---

[46] See Philippians 2:12

20:7 Just as the prophet spoke, saying, "When my soul was separated from my flesh, my Lord, you knew my path. They had hid a trap for me on my path and I saw them returning to the right. I lacked one who knows me and I have nothing whereby I can escape."[47] For they take us into darkness, and cannot see their faces.

20:8 Since he knows that the demons ridicule him, and lead him down the path he does not know, he will speak this. And if he returns, to the left or to the right, there is no man who knows him.

20:9 He is alone amongst the demons, yet there are none who know him.

20:10 The subtlety of the angels of light are sent to those righteous people, that they might receive their souls, and take them to the place of light, towards the garden, where their prosperity is found.

20:11 Demons and angels of darkness are those who are sent forth to receive and take them towards Gehenna, that was prepared for them, so that they might receive their punishment for the sins of their hands.

20:12 Woe for all sinners' souls who are taken towards destruction, who have no comfort or rest. They cannot escape from the punishment that they are found in, nor leave Gehenna for all eternity.

20:13 For they have abided in the work of Cain, and they have perished for the cost of Balaam's iniquity. They have omission in what they do. Woe to sinners, for they are among those who commit usury, so that might take the money of aliens violently. They will receive their punishment in Gehenna for the sins of their hands.

20:14 They shall receive their punishment in Gehenna for the sins of their hands.

---

[47] This appears to be Ps. 142:3-6

CHAPTER XXI

21:1 Where are those people who collect the money of aliens, that was not the work of her hands, nor truly their money?

21:2 They freely take a person's money, and they shall be gathered without their knowing on the day of their death, that will arrive there. However, they will leave their money for a foreigner.

21:3 Just as their fathers, they are the kin of sinners who are worrisome and take hold of sinners through theft and robbery, so that their children cannot be joyful with their father's money.

21:4 Since they have gathered them together in violence, they will become like the vapor of urine, and like the smoke that the wind scatters, and like that of the wilting grass., and like wax that melts in the fire, for all sinners' glory will perish as this. There is no one whom will benefit from the money of their father, just as David spoke saying, "I saw a sinner

21:5 being honored in fame with flowers and cypress[48], but when I returned, I missed him. I searched for him and did not find his place." There is no one who will benefit from their father's money.

21:6 Since they have gathered their wealth in violence, they believe they are impervious. Just as those men who wrong their companions do not boast, the destruction of sinners happens at once.

21:7 You slothful ones, know that you will perish and that your wealth will perish with you. If you have a bounty of silver and gold, it will rust.

21:8 If you have many progeny, you will also have many graves. If you have many houses, they will be leveled,

---

[48] Perhaps Ps. 73, although this is unclear

21:9   for you did not do the will of the Lord. If you have livestock that multiplied, they shall be taken by your enemies, and all of the wealth you seized with your hands will not be found. It has not been blessed.

21:10   Whether it is in a house or a forest, a wilderness or a meadow, a winepress or a threshing floor, it will not be found.

21:11   Since you did not keep the command of the Lord, the Lord will not save you or your household from the judgment. There will be melancholy when your enemies arise, yet you will not rejoice in the children of your own house.

21:12   From the bounty of [the Lord], He will not trouble those who keep His law and His orders. He will give of all who ask of Him. He will bless the children of those houses, and also the fruit of the land for them.

21:13   He makes them sovereign upon all the peoples in their nation, that they might rule over them all. He gives them everything, His bounty in the land of pasture.

21:14   He blesses all those things they hold in their hands, all their fields of grain, and all their fields of livestock. He makes them rejoice in their children born of their own house.

21:15   He will not lower the number of their livestock. He will save them all from the judgment, and from weakness, sickness, and destruction. As well as from the enemies that they know, and those they do not know.

21:16   He will stand in defense of them at the time of judgment, and He will save them from evil things, and from their enemies, and from tribulation. In ancient days, when a priest abode in a tent and kept the law and order of the bedouin, living faithfully in the law of the Lord, by the primary command of the law, they would give him his tithe, bringing forth the first born amongst their livestock. He will offer them His salvation.

21:17 Just as Moses commanded Joshua son of Nun, that there must be a city of sanctuary in every nation, so that they will not know until the day of judgment, who was convicted and who was acquitted,

21:18 for if a living man has killed a soul, he will be judged there so that he might be saved.

21:19 He said to them, "Look into your heart to those who you have previously quarreled. Be it by axe or be it by stone or by wood, as it unknowingly fell from his hand. If he says 'that person from whom it falls will die,' see him and save him, for if he does not know his deeds, he must be saved.

21:20 Yet, if he is aware, he will receive punishment for his sin, and there will be no clemency for him. If murder is committed, by accident, since he is unaware, he will be examined and saved from his death."

21:21 [The Lord] sought them out so that they might be separate from their sin. Moses would work likewise for the children of Israel, so that they would not depart from the law of the Lord.

21:22 He commanded them that the children of Adam who abide faithfully in the commands of the Lord, avoiding the worship of idols, and not eating what was illicit and had been cut by the sword, and distancing themselves from evil deeds and those who work them, so that they might be commit themselves to distancing themselves from what is due to them.

21:23 [The Lord] ordered them, lest they depart from His command. He committed them in the tabernacle as an example of heaven, so that they might save their bodies, and might reside with their fathers.

21:24 Since they have been born of Seth and Adam, who did the will of the Lord, and who believed in the word or the Lord, abiding faithfully in His commands, they will be called the children of righteousness.

21:25   As they are Adam's children, and He has created them in His image[49] and appearance, they might do good deeds so that the Lord might rejoice, and will not scorn them.

21:26   [The Lord] will not separate his friends, if they are righteous. They will inherit the Kingdom of Heaven, where those who are committed to righteousness abide.

21:27   [The Lord] loves all those who ask of Him with a clean heart, and He hears their prayers. He accepts the penance of the disciplined. He gives strength and power to those who keep His law, His order, and His command.

21:28   Those who did His will will rejoice with Him in the kingdom forever, whether they are those from before or who rose at some later time. They will praise Him from that day until the infinite age.

Give glory to the Lord forever, and with this the second [book] of Maccabees is completed and fulfilled.

---

[49] See Gen. 1:27

The Scriptorium Project is the work of a small group of lay people of various apostolic churches who are interested in the preservation, transmission, and translation of the works of the early and medieval church. Our efforts are to make the works of the church fathers accessible to anyone who might have an interest in Christian antiquities and the theological, philosophical, and moral writings that have become the bedrock of Western Civilization.

To-date, our releases have pulled from the Greek, Syriac, Georgian, Latin, Celtic, Ethiopian, and Coptic traditions of Christianity, and have been pulled from sundry local traditions and languages.

www.ingramcontent.com/pod-product-compliance
Lightning Source LLC
LaVergne TN
LVHW052005060526
838201LV00059B/3844